Major John Scott

Major Scott's Speech in the House of Commons

On the 1st and 3d of July 1789 Upon the State and Finances of India

Major John Scott

Major Scott's Speech in the House of Commons
On the 1st and 3d of July 1789 Upon the State and Finances of India

ISBN/EAN: 9783337059156

Printed in Europe, USA, Canada, Australia, Japan

Cover: Foto ©Suzi / pixelio.de

More available books at **www.hansebooks.com**

Major SCOTT's

SPEECH

IN THE

HOUSE OF COMMONS,

On the 1st and 3d of July 1789;

UPON THE

STATE and FINANCES of INDIA.

Her

———————

LONDON:

PRINTED FOR JOHN STOCKDALE, OPPOSITE
BURLINGTON-HOUSE, PICCADILLY.

MDCCLXXXIX.

[Price One Shilling.]

Wednesday, July 1.

MR. DUNDAS moved to refer the Papers and Accounts presented from the India House to a Committee of the whole House.

The Motion being agreed to, the House resolved itself into the said Committee, Lord Frederick Campbell in the Chair,

Mr. Dundas opened the Budget; and afterwards concluded with moving,

" That it appears to this Committee, that
" the annual revenues of the East India Company
" in the provinces of Bengal, Bahar, and Oriſſa,
" and from Benares and Oude, under the heads
" of mint or coinage duties, post-office collections,
" Benares revenue, Oude subſidy, land revenues,
" customs, and the receipts from the sales of salt
" and opium, amount, on the average of three

" years,

" years, from 1785-6 to 1787-8, both inclusive,
" to the sum of five crore eight lacks eighty-
" seven thousand six hundred and fifty-five cur-
" rent rupees."

LORD FREDERICK CAMPBELL,

I RISE with a peculiar degree of satisfaction
and pleasure, to offer a few remarks to the
House, on the day expressly appointed for taking
into consideration the past and present state of
the British Government in India.

It is highly honourable to the King's Ministers, that they do now, for a third time, bring
fairly and fully forward, to the view of Parliament and the Public, the actual state of that
distant Empire.

It has been my warmest wish, my Lord, at
all times, to detect and expose those most falla-
cious and ridiculous accounts which have been
detailed in this House, and elsewhere; and dif-
feminated with so much industry throughout
this nation, and throughout Europe; relative to
the state of Bengal, and its dependencies. Gentlemen

men are well aware, that where two reprefenta-
tions of the fituation of a whole people are
given, totally differing from each other in every
particular, both cannot be true, Thofe who fit
oppofite to me, have for fome years paft been
in the habit of defcribing the natives of Bengal
and its dependencies, as reduced to the loweft
ftate of depreffion, mifery, and fubjection; the
people fleeced of their property; the revenues
collected with a degree of feverity, at which
humanity fhudders; wanton oppreffion, grofs
injuftice, deliberate unprovoked tyranny,
marking every act of the Britifh Government;
and the fyftem eftablifhed at home, exprefsly
calculated to perpetuate thofe miferies, which
it profeffed to remedy. This is no exaggera-
tion: thofe who have attended to the debates of
this Houfe, or to proceedings elfewhere,
well know, that our language has been ran-
facked for epithets fufficiently forcible to con-
demn every part of the prefent fyftem. I will not
again allude to the dreadful tales that have been
told—tales which this Houfe knows now, have
no foundation in truth, but by which I will
confidently affirm, that Parliament and the na-

tion

tion have been degraded, diſhonóured, and diſgraced in the eyes of all Europe. Were they believed, thoſe humane and liberal-minded men, who without further enquiry would have aboliſhed much of the important commerce of this country, muſt, I am ſure, have long ago propoſed to withdraw every Engliſhman from Indoſtan. This Houſe has now every poſſible means of information before them, and I know that the gentlemen who ſit oppoſite to me, are not ignorant of the true ſtate of Bengal. For what purpoſe is it then, that the national character continues to be degraded throughout the world? Is the voice of calumny to be inceſſantly employed, becauſe thoſe who ſerved their country in India had the good fortune to do, what many who were employed elſewhere could not accompliſh? But I have too much confidence in the honour and the good ſenſe of this Houſe, to think that gentlemen will ſhut their ears to conviction. I will not preſume to advance one word which I cannot ſupport, either by evidence upon your table now, or by evidence that can at any moment be called to your bar. Nay, I would even venture to appeal to

the

the Hon. Gentleman oppofite to me (Mr. Sheri-
dan), to prove the fallacy of thofe accounts which
have been fo confidently delivered, fince that
gentleman has a general acquaintance, and has
other means of information, by which he muft
know how grofsly erroneous all the ftatements
have been, that were given from gentlemen on
that fide of the Houfe, as to Bengal, Benares,
or Oude.

An Hon. Gentleman (Mr. Francis), whom
I do not now fee in his place (Mr. Francis
juft then walked up the Houfe), but whom I
this inftant have the pleafure to behold, that
Hon. Gentleman, for the firft time that an India budget has been opened, has omitted to fay
one word as to the ftate of the government of
India, or to reprobate, as he ufed to do, the
fyftem under which it was governed. This I
take to be a good omen, and I hope we fhall
all agree in the end.

Twenty-five years have elapfed fince this nation has poffeffed an abfolute fovereignty over
one of the fineft and the moft populous king-

doms

doms of the earth. It was our policy for the
firft feven years of the period to leave the en-
tire government of the country in the hands of
one Mahomedan ; but from the year 1772 to the
prefent moment, the government of the country, the collections of the revenues, and the
adminiftration of juftice, have been in the hands
of the Englifh themfelves; and I affirm it to
be a truth uncontroverted, incontrovertible,
never difputed by any difintereſted man of common fenfe, that from 1772 to the prefent hour,
Bengal has been in a rapid ftate of improvement, with refpect to agriculture, population,
and commerce. The King's Minifters, and thofe
who have accefs to the beft official information,
admit the truth of this fact. It is confirmed
by the folemn declaration of every gentleman
who arrives from Bengal. It is proved by the
productivenefs of the revenue, and by the afto-
nifhing drains which that country has borne
during the late arduous ftruggle for exiftence
in India; and yet, my Lord, the fact has not
only been denied in this Houfe, but the authority and the name of the Houfe are ufed in diffe-
minating to the world the moft folemn decla-
rations,

rations, that by mal-adminiftration " the wel-
" fare of the Eaft India Company has mate-
" rially fuffered, the happinefs of the natives
" of India been deeply affected, their confi-
" dence in Englifh faith and lenity fhaken
" and impaired, and the honour of the Crown,
" and character of this nation, wantonly and
" wickedly degraded.".

Such is one of the melancholy reprefenta-
tions which this Houfe has nominally fanctioned.
Let any gentleman read what the Houfe has
faid relative to the mode by which the revenues
of Bengal have been for years, and are at this
very moment, collected. If I am to believe
what this Houfe has folemnly declared to be
true, I muft fay that the revenues have been
and are collected in a manner " vexatious, op-
" preffive, and deftructive to the inhabitants
" of Bengal; and that the rights of private
" property have been moft notorioufly and
" fcandaloufly violated." If the defcription of
the internal government of Bengal is thus melancholy, it is fo in a ftill greater degree as we
advance upon the Ganges. Gentlemen have

B   all

all heard the ftate and condition of Benares and of Oude, as defcribed both in and out of the Houfe, and as defcribed in the name and by the authority of the Houfe. Let me, therefore now proceed, from unqueftionable evidence, to do away this load of grofs and foolifh mifreprefentation, which, though it may advance the views and defigns of a faction, degrades us in the eye of the Public.

I fhall in no cafe now prefume to quote the authority of that Gentleman whom this Houfe has thought proper to impeach ; but I have an undoubted right to quote as complete evidence, the folemn declaration of his immediate fucceffor (Sir John Macpherfon). On the 10th of Auguft 1786, Sir John writes as follows to the Court of Directors :—" The condition in which Earl " Cornwallis will receive the government of " India, is creditable to the Company, and " cannot but be fatisfactory to the nation. The " native inhabitants of this kingdom are, I be- " lieve, the happieft, and the beft protected " fubjects in India ; our native allies and tri- " butaries are fatisfied, and confide in our pro-

9   " tection;

" tection; the country powers are emuloufly
" afpiring to the friendfhip of the Englifh; and
" from the King of Tidore towards New Gui-
" nea, to Timur Shaw on the banks of the In-
" dus, there is not a ftate that has not lately
" given us proofs of confidence and refpect."—
I will not pay fo fulfome a compliment to Sir
John Macpherfon (whofe merits I am as ready
as any man to acknowledge) as to fay, that this
happinefs of the natives, this refpect and confidence of foreign powers, was the confequence of
any meafure recently purfued. The fact is, my
Lord, that the Britifh name then, and for years
before, ftood high in India; and that the natives of Bengal were then, as they had been for
years before, " the happieft and the beft pro-
" tected fubjects in India."

Another Gentleman who has long ferved the
Company in very important offices, and now
fills, with great credit to himfelf, and advantage
to the Company, one of the firft offices it has to
beftow (I mean Mr. Shore), faid in the year
1781, " That the natives were happier, and
" their property better fecured under our
" government, than under that of their for-

B 2   " mer

" mer fovereigns. This," fays Mr. Shore,
" I fpeak with all the confidence convic-.
" tion infpires." The fame Gentleman de-
fended the government of Bengal in the laft
year, when it was afferted that feverities ufed in
a diftant province to compel the payment of
balances were common in Bengal. The fact
was pofitively denied, whatever might have
been the practice in a remote corner of a diftant
province. This was faid when the charges
preferred againft Deby Sing were finally deter-
mined upon ; and, for the honour of the Britifh
nation, I truft the time will come when that
ftory fhall be fully invuftigated in this Houfe.

My Lord, the next document to which I fhall
refer, in proof of the profperous ftate of Bengal,
is a very curious letter from Mr. James Grant to
Earl Cornwallis, now upon your table. A more
authentic, or a more conclufive document, cannot be produced. Salt is a neceffary of life in
all countries, but more particularly fo in Bengal,
where fome of the Cafts eat no flefh meat, others
very little, and where falt is confumed by all.
Mr. Grant has had accefs to every official document, and to every other channel of information,

tion, neceſſary to elucidate the ſubject on which
he writes; and he has proved, that the conſumption of ſalt in 1780 was conſiderably more than
a third beyond the conſumption of the ſame article in 1765. He then adds, " A lapſe of
" fifteen years under the lenity of the Engliſh
" government, had certainly operated a very
" material change in the ſtate of things. Greater
" ſecurity and freedom in agriculture, manu-
" factures, and commerce, increaſed conſider-
" ably the population of the country, with the
" wealth and the proſperity of its inhabitants.
" An additional conſumption of all the neceſ-
" ſaries of life was a natural conſequence, and
" fully evinced the improved condition of the
" Britiſh provinces."

In another part of his Letter, Mr. Grant ſtates
this as " indicating with moral, infallible cer-
" tainty, a prodigious increaſe of population, and
" all its concomitant advantages, in a period of
" little more than twenty years." And arguing
from the data he has laid down, Mr. Grant
ſuppoſes the inhabitants under the Bengal government to be thirteen millions ſix hundred
thou-

thousand souls. The Letter is before the House, and I refer Gentlemen to it as a most valuable and curious document. It is decisive as to the point for which I moved for it, which was to shew the improved and the improving state of Bengal under the British government. This Gentleman was appointed to a very considerable office under the Bengal government, not by Mr. Haftings, but by Sir John Macpherson.— His character stands high and unimpeached.— His affiduity is unremitted—and I am thoroughly convinced of the truth of his statement, and of the justice of the conclusions which he draws from it,

The same Gentleman has written an Analysis of the Revenues of Bengal, Bahar, Oriffa, the Northern Circars, and Benares. They are very voluminous, and contain much valuable information, all tending to confirm most fully every thing that I have had the honour at any time to state to this House—in particular, the Analysis of the Benares Revenues states, that forty lacks is a very moderate annual affeffment, and utterly does away every affertion that has

been

been made by gentlemen oppofite to me, relative to the ftate of that diftrict, or the rights of
of its zemindars.—It is not from difrefpect to
Mr. Grant that I have not moved for them to be
laid upon·the table. I ·underftand he will be
foon in England; and if he can prove to the fa-
tisfaction of the Right Hon. Gentleman below
me (Mr. Dundas), that the zemindars of Bengal,
and the native officers, have defrauded government annually of a million a year for twenty-
five years, I dare fay he would be very happy to
bring that fum hereafter into the exchequer.

My Lord, in addition to Mr. Grant's authority, I can quote the fentiments of every Englifh
Gentleman who has left Bengal in the feven laft
years, and particularly a Gentleman of great
knowledge and obfervation, who was twelve
years beyond the Company's provinces. That
Gentleman (Colonel Polier, who is lately ar-
rived) affured me, that in paffing from the
banks of the Carumnaffa, which divides Bahar
from the province of Benares, down to Cal-
cutta, about 520 miles, he faw a country improved

proved beyond what he conceived was possible in such a space of time.

The next evidence that I shall adduce, comes most materially and pointedly to the fact; I mean the Testimonials transmitted by all the principal natives of Bengal and its dependencies, relative to Warren Hastings Esq. late Governor General of Bengal. If Gentlemen opposite to me will give no credit to the King's ministers, nor to Earl Cornwallis, nor Sir John Macpherson, nor Mr. Grant; if they will not believe the solemn assertions of every English gentleman who arrives from the country; if they continue to this moment to affirm that Bengal is ruined, exhausted, and desolated; I hope they will alter their language after they have heard what the natives themselves say, from the highest to the lowest ranks amongst them, and *that* uncontrovertible evidence is now upon the table of this House. The manner in which these Testimonials have been sent home eludes every possibility of suspicion as to their authenticity. It is a fact of universal notoriety,

notoriety, that the natives were eager, and
anxious to fhew their refpect for the Britifh
government ; to declare the happinefs which
they enjoyed under the protection of the man,
who for thirteen years had been placed over
them ; and who, in point of fact, firft reduced
that government into fyftem. That thefe Tefti-
monials are highly important to the Gentleman
of whom they make fuch diftinguifhed and
honourable mention is certain; but to this
Houfe, on this day, they are alfo important,
in fo far as they fully confirm all that Sir John
Macpherfon, Mr. Grant, Mr. Shore, the King's
Minifters, and every unbiaffed well-informed
perfon has faid, of the fuperiority of the Englifh
government in India, over that of any native
adminiftration whatever. What is faid upon
this fubject by one man is fo peculiarly ftriking,
that I fhall beg leave to repeat it. Meer Afh-
ruff Dean Hofemy, who figns the Patna addrefs, adds after his name thefe words : " From
" the juftice of Mr. Haftings, his protection
" of the people, and his excellent conduct to-
" wards them ; the people of other countries
" defired, as for example thofe of Cafhmier
C " lift

" lift up their hands in prayer, that God would
" make the Englifh government the lot of
" their country."

Having now, my Lord, laid this ground
work, I fhall refer to my laft evidence, which
binds and fixes the whole; I mean, the eftimated and actual receipts of revenue under the
Bengal government for one complete year. The
eftimated revenue for 1787-8, was five millions
fixty-four thoufand eight hundred and ninety
pounds twelve fhillings; but the actual revenue received was five millions one hundred
and eighty-two thoufand feven hundred and
eighty pounds; the eftimated expences were
three millions fixty-fix thoufand pounds; the
actual expences were three millions forty-fix
thoufand pounds; fo that, from the receipts
and expences of Bengal, defcribed by fome
Gentlemen as oppreffed, ruined, and depo-
pulated; there was in the laft year a real available furplus in Bengal of revenue, beyond expences of every denomination, of two millions
one hundred and thirty-five thoufand nine hundred and thirty pounds, confiderably exceeding
the

the furplus which it was eftimated the laft year
would afford. Whether this furplus has been
wifely difpofed of, by paying it away in part to
Madras, or Bombay ; whether the Military
Eftablifhments there fo far beyond their means
of paying ought, or ought not to be reduced,
is no part of my argument; for on this day I
wifh to confine myfelf to Bengal, and to fhew,
that there is no other country upon earth that
can boaft of fuch a furplus revenue; that there
is no country more flourifhing, nor body of
people more happy or contented. The Right
Honourable Gentleman who opened the Budget
contented himfelf with merely ftating the amount
of the receipts and expenditure, but with the
leave of the Houfe I fhall fay a few words
upon the moft material items. The firft is the
Benares revenue. Gentlemen will fee that more
than the eftimated revenue is actually received.
The total, above forty-five lacks of rupees.
Does the Right Honourable Gentleman, or any
other perfon, exprefs the leaft doubt as to the
collections of future years? On the contrary,
does not Mr. Grant, a well-informed man and
a clear authority, fay, that the affeffment is

moderate ?

moderate? How is that to be reconciled with what this Houfe has faid as to Benares? How is it to be reconciled with what the reprefentatives of this Houfe have faid elfewhere, relative to the ftate and fituation of that valuable, and flourifhing province? This Houfe has pronounced that country to be totally ruined, and defolated. Deftrustion, devaftation, and oppreffion, are the epithets ufed by this Houfe in defcribing the ftate of that. country at no very diftant period. The defcription, I confidently affirm, is not true; becaufe the Houfe knows, that from a country fo defcribed, no revenues could be collested. The fums received, and the united voice of the natives, are a fufficient refutation of fo gloomy an account. So far from the revenue which Mr. Haftings fixed in 1781 falling fhort, it is likely to increafe, from the addition of the opium, which Earl Cornwallis has taken for the benefit of the Company.

The next article is the Oude fubfidy, above five hundred and twenty-five thoufand pounds, of which at the end of the year the trifling
balance

balance of. five thoufand five hundred pounds
only remained. Will Gentlemen have the
goodnefs to recollect for one moment, what
has been faid in this Houfe relative to Oude ?
Do they' not remember, that when a Right Honourable Gentleman (Mr. Fox) brought in his
celebrated India Bill, there, was a balance of
above 'feven hundred thoufand pounds due to
.the Company from Oude ? Do they not remember, that by one dafh of the pen he ftruck
out the whole ? Yet, fince that period, the
whole has been paid. By papers before this
Houfe, we know that eight millions fterling
was received from Oude in eight years ; and
that by the prefent arrangement the Nabob pays more than the third of the expence
of our army. But is there a man in the kingdom who gives credit to the accounts which he
has heard, or the articles we have voted, who
will not fay, that inftead of receiving half a million annually from Oude, we ought, for years
to come, to fend half a million a year into that
country ? And here let me ferioufly call the attention of Gentlemen to a fact, which I have
often mentioned before, but which cannot be
noticed

noticed too often. This Houfe paffed thirteen
articles relative to Oude, but did not, and could
not read them, as I can prove from a reference
to the Journals. In thofe articles, the prefent
fyftem, by which Oude is connected with Bengal, is condemned in all its parts. The Mini-
fter, Hyder Beg Khan, is termed, in thofe articles, "an implacable tyrant," and the power
with which Mr. Haftings invefted him, is ftated
to be monftrous, and the act itfelf highly cri-
minal. Will the Houfe be pleafed to hear what
Earl Cornwallis and the Directors, under the
fanction of the King's Minifters, fay as to the
fyftem by which Oude is governed ?

Lord Cornwallis fays, 20th April 1787,
" The only material difference which has taken
" place in the engagements between this go-
" vernment and the Nabob Vizier, relates to
" the brigade ftationed in Futtyghur ; the con-
" tinuance of which body of troops in the do-
" minions of the Vizier I deem equally effen-
" tial to the intereft of the Vizier and the
" Company. In other refpects I have nearly
" adhered to the principles eftablifhed by the
" former

" former Governor General, Mr. Haftings,
" and fince confirmed by the orders of the
" Honourable the Court of Directors. All the
" fubfidiary arrangements have been formed
" with a view to ftrengthen thofe principles,
" and render them permanent."

So late as the 8th of April laft, this communi-
nication is replied to by the Directors, and the
King's Minifters, as follows:

" Having attentively perufed all the minutes,
" proceedings, and letters, referred to in thefe
" paragraphs, and in your fubfequent advices
" on the fubject of the late agreement, con-
" cluded by Lord Cornwallis with the Vizier,
" we approve of the general arrangement, and
" of the principles on which it was formed."

How, my Lord, is this decided approba-
tion, and the continuance of. the .fyftem, with
the full knowledge of this Houfe, to be reconciled with our permitting thofe articles to which
I allude to remain upon our Journals? I fhall
pufh the fubject no farther.

In

In Bengal, Gentlemen will fee, that the revenues from land, falt, and opium are much
beyond the eftimate: the two latter were in fact
created by Mr. Haftings himfelf, and produce
confiderably more than half a million a year.
And here, my Lord, I defire to call the attention of the Houfe to another curious fact. If
Gentlemen will look to the total revenues of
Bengal, including Benares and Oude, in the laft
ten years, they will find a very remarkable
and wonderful equality in them; the difference
not more than eight or ten thoufand pounds.
And when it is confidered that above five millions fterling a year have been received, the difference in each year's receipts bear no proportion to that difference which every Gentleman of landed property in this Houfe feels in
proportion to the amount of his income, either
from the failure of tenants, or the repairs of
farm houfes. In point of fact, during the
whole of the late war, the refources of the Bengal government were equal to what they now
are; or how could we have fo fuccefsfully re-
fifted the whole world? During that war, Bengal fupplied Madras and Bombay with above

feven

seven millions sterling in money and provisions;
and it has sent immense sums, since the peace,
to liquidate arrears, and to pay establishments.
The more Gentlemen go to the bottom of this
subject, the more they will be convinced that I
have never deceived them in any statements.

I have now, my Lord, endeavoured to state,
and as concisely as possible, the actual state of
Bengal, Benares, and Oude, under a system so
strongly, and allow me to add, so absurdly reprobated in all its parts. No Gentleman in or
out of this House can entertain a more exalted
opinion of Lord Cornwallis than I do, or can
feel a stronger sense of the important services
that he has rendered; nor will any fair and can-
did man withhold, either from the Board of
Controul or the Directors, the applause which
they so justly merit. But I will not so far of-
fend against common sense as to say, that the
flourishing and prosperous state of Bengal is
owing exclusively to measures which they have
pursued. For the œconomical arrangements
that they have established, and which Earl Cornwallis has so vigorously enforced, every praise is

D   due;

due; but the fact I wish to imprefs fo ftrongly upon the Houfe is this; that in *the fyftem* no alteration has been made. In Oude, as Lord Cornwallis tells you, the fyftem eftablifhed by Mr. Haftings is adhered to; fo at Furrukabad; fo with Fyzoola Cawn; Benares the fame. Full credit is taken for all the fums collected from thefe countries, and the fyftem is continued. In Bengal there is no alteration. Mr. Shore, who is at the head of the revenues under Lord Cornwallis, was in the fame fituation under Mr. Haftings. Zemindars in fome inftances, farmers in others, collect the revenues now as they did when Mr. Haftings was there. Salt and opium form two great branches of the public revenue; both in fact created by Mr. Haftings. Juftice is adminiftered now as it was when he was there. The inland cuftoms only have been abolifhed, and the Houfe knows that Mr. Haftings recommended the abolition of them many years ago. To enfure the continuance of profperity in Bengal, this Houfe, againft the moft vehement and continued oppofition of the Gentlemen oppofite to me, conferred additional powers on the Governor General. I then pre-

dicted

8

dicted the happy effects which that falutary law would produce, and we now experience them in the higheft degree.

I remember, when I fat in the gallery in the laft parliament, that a Right Hon. Gentleman (Mr. Fox), who but the year before had defcribed the miferable ftate of the Britifh navy, took occafion to ftate it as highly flourifhing, under the unremitting attention of the then Firft Lord of the Admiralty (Lord Keppel). A noble Lord (North) very properly obferved in reply, that fhips could not fpring up like mufhrooms: that infinite credit was due to the late Lord (Sandwich), though that Right Hon. Gentleman propofed to the Houfe to addrefs his Majefty to remove him from his councils ; and he might fay to the prefent Lord, "Alexander has conquer-" ed with the foldiers of Philip." So it is in Bengal; the profperous ftate of that country has not been the work of a day, nor of a year, but it has been in a progreffive ftate of improvement under the mild influence of the Britifh Government for a feries of years, until it is now become, as a Right Hon. Gentleman (Mr. Dundas) fo emphatically deemed it, the brighteft jewel in the Britifh Crown.

Friday, July 3.

Mr. Speaker,

AFTER having trespassed so long upon the indulgence of the House the other night, I shall only now presume to detain them a few minutes, in consequence of what fell from an honourable and respectable Gentleman (Mr. Dempster), whose good opinion I am very anxious to retain, and who I wish should think well of every part of our Indian government. Though I have no encouragement to add to my former observations, from the present appearance of the House, yet it convinces me of one thing, that what I did take the liberty to say, *cannot be answered*; for if the gentlemen who were formerly so loud in opposition to the line I have taken, could defend or support *their former assertions*, they would not be absent on this day;—nor would another set of gentlemen

be

be filent, if they had not difcovered their former errors.—Is it poffible, Mr. Speaker, that
thofe gentlemen who would abolifh a valuable
commerce, on the very appearance only of its
being oppreffive, would fit filent on a fubjeĉt
where the happinefs of millions is at ftake,
unlefs they knew how grofsly they had been
deceived? For I never can imprefs this truth
too ftrongly upon this Houfe and the Public,—
*That the fyftem by which Bengal is governed at this
prefent moment, is precifely the fyftem that ftands fo
ftrikingly condemned by the Votes, and upon the
Journals of this Houfe.*

The Honourable Gentleman finds fault with
the large military eftablifhment in Bengal; but
I beg he will recolleĉt the prodigious extent of
country which our army covers and defends;
—twelve hundred and fifty miles in length, and
in fome places fix hundred and fifty in breadth.
I would alfo defire the Honourable Gentlemen to
recolleĉt, that more than one-third of the expence of the Bengal army is borne by the Nabob
of Oude, whofe country, in return, is effeĉtually
fecured. I alfo call to the recolleĉtion of the
Honour-

Honourable Gentleman, that this great fubfidy
is regularly paid; that, in eight years of our
greateft difficulty, we received eight millions
fterling from Oude. I am fure he will remember too, that a Right Honourable Gentleman
(Mr. Fox), a few years ago, ftruck our,
with one dafh of his pen, above feven
hundred and twenty thoufand pounds, then
owing by the Vizur to the Company. Every
rupee has long ago been paid. And here I in-
form that Hon. Gentleman that *the fyftem* by
which Oude is connected with Bengal, is *precifely that fyftem* which *Mr. Haftings eftablifhed*.
Lord Cornwallis tells the Company, that in his
fubfidiary arrangements, if he has made any
alterations, it is *with a view to ftrengthen thofe
principles, and to render them more permanent*.
The Court of Directors, and the King's Minifters, *approve this fyftem* in their reply to Lord
Cornwallis, *and the principles on which it was
formed*. If the Houfe was better attended, Mr.
Speaker, I fhould have much to fay upon this
fubject, but I leave it to Gentlemen to compare
this account, with what the Houfe has done,
and what has been faid in its name elfewhere.

There

There is another point on which I beg to set the Hon. Gentleman right. He does not think so large an eftablifhment of Sepoys neceffary, and fays, our great dependance muft be upon an European force in time of danger! Here I totally differ from the Hon. Gentleman; and though I am as much an advocate for a refpectable European force in India as he can poffibly be, yet the real effective force for fervice in India ever has been, and ever muft be, our Sepoy battalions. We have brought them to fuch a degree of perfection in point of difcipline, as ftrikes every Englifh officer who fees them, for the firft time, with aftonifhment; and in the late war, one of our Bengal battalions of Sepoys came to the pufh of the bayonet with a veteran French regiment, and actually repulfed it. Their attachment to us is fo great, that during the late war when they were fix, feven, and eight months in arrears, at a time that they had fold their filver ornaments for fubfiftence, no mutiny happened, though fuch an event was with great reafon apprehended.

The

The Hon. Gentleman has expreſſed his wiſh
that the monopoly of opium may be aboliſhed;
and he has told the Houſe a very dreadful ſtory
of corn having been ploughed up, and poppies
planted in its ſtead; I heard that ſtory above
eighteen years ago, but from very particular
enquiry, have great reaſon to believe it was not
true. It was ſaid to have been done in the
year 1769. But whether true or not, the trade
has been regulated for a great number of years;
and ſuch a thing can never happen. Opium
ever has been, and ever muſt be, a monopoly.
Mr. Haſtings made that, as well as ſalt, an
article of revenue for the Company; and it is
highly important to the export trade of Cal-
cutta.

I believe, Mr. Speaker, theſe are the only
objections which the Honourable Gentleman
made to the ſtatement; and I deſire to call to
the recollection of this Houſe, thin as it is,
that, by the reſolution now in your hand, we
are going to take credit for an immenſe revenue in Bengal, all of it acquired by means
which this Houſe, in another character, has

condemned; all of it retained under a fyftem which this Houfe, in another place, has, by its Reprefentatives, ftrongly reprobated.

With regard to the eftablifhments of Madras and Bombay, fo much beyond their ability to pay, I think they ought to be reduced upon this principle (fince a Right Honourable Gentleman [Mr. Dundas] has particularly applied to me), that we fhall not be able to keep them up: that Bengal cannot bear an annual drain of fifty lacks to Bombay, and twenty to Madras; therefore, I would leffen the eftablifh-ments there, and increafe them in Bengal; for this very obvious reafon; becaufe, if the efta-blifhments are kept up in Bengal, Govern-ment pays with one hand, and receives with the other. But money, circulating fpecie, fent to Madras and Bombay, is loft for ever to Ben-gal. Marine battalions raifed in Bengal would, in my opinion, be ready for foreign fervice, and keep our fpecie in Bengal. If, however, the Right Honourable Gentleman thinks he can fpare fifty lacks to Madras, and twenty to Bombay, after all the drains Bengal has fuf-fered,

fered, every argument I have ufed is ftrength-
ened in the higheft degree, and the former
adminiftration deferves even more credit than
I have given to it.

THE END.

www.ingramcontent.com/pod-product-compliance
Lightning Source LLC
Chambersburg PA
CBHW021605270326
41931CB00009B/1376